KINSHIP WITH GO

HEAVEN IS AT YOUR MOTHER'S FEET

DAUGHTERS OF AFRICA

STRUGGLE FOR EXISTENCE

RHYTHM OF BEAUTY

A REGENERATIVE FORCE

ORACLE OF MY HEART

LEADING US TO THE SUNRISE

KINSHIP WITH GOD

HEAVEN IS AT YOUR MOTHER'S FEET

DAUGHTERS OF AFRICA

STRUGGLE FOR EXISTENCE

RHYTHM OF BEAUTY

A REGENERATIVE FORCE

ORACLE OF MY HEART

LEADING US TO THE SUNRISE

BLACK WOMEN

image

IN THE IMAGE OF GOD

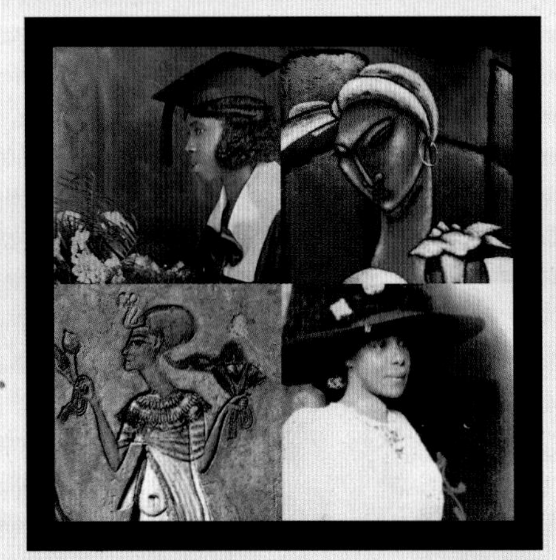

EDITED BY DOROTHY WINBUSH RILEY

IN THE IMAGE OF GOD

The Pilgrim Press, Cleveland, Ohio 44115

Printed in China on acid-free paper

04 03 02 01 00 99 5 4 3 2 1

Library of Congress Cataloging-in-Publication Data
Black women in the image of God / edited by Dorothy Winbush Riley.
p. cm.
ISBN 0-8298-1257-1 (pbk. : alk. paper)
1. Afro-American women—Quotations, maxims, etc. 2. Afro-American women—Pictorial works.
I. Riley, D. Winbush (Dorothy Winbush)
E185.86.B5425 1999
305.48'896073—dc21 98-50324
CIP

CONTENTS

ACKNOWLEDGMENTS

My greatest thanks go to:

Ted Riley, my son, who was the reason this book for African American men was envisioned. Ted, I love you and I am proud of your accomplishments. Stay centered and focused with the knowledge that your strength is from the Creator.

Tiaudra Riley, my daughter, who inspired me to create a book for African American women that was as beautiful as the one for men, who wisely encouraged me with wisdom unusual in one so young.

Schiavi Riley, my firstborn, who looks at me with awe, then questions what I do so that I stay grounded and real. I marvel at your talent and perseverance—when you decide to complete a task, it is done.

Martay Fleming, my nephew, and Nandi Riley, my granddaughter, whose questioning eyes motivated me to complete each book.

Special thanks for art go to:

Brenda Stroud, Elwyn Bush, and Donald Calloway, who opened their private collections to me; the generous spirits of Jonathan Green (Naples, Florida), Mike Colt (Los Angeles), Earl Jackson (Ann Arbor), Sophia LaCroix (Miami), and La Shun Beal (Houston), who became supporters and friends in creating this book.

Special thanks for poetry go to:

Judy Griffie, writer, whose genuine support, love, and understanding of the circle of love bonds us as kindred spirits.

Naomi Long Madgett, poet, whose love of writing and kind words inspired me through the years to have the courage to write and to be published.

Special thanks to Pilgrim Press and its associates go to:

Kim Sadler, my editor, who understood my desire and shaped this volume from more than three hundred pages and photographs.

Martha Clark, art director, who designed the book and made each page a marvel to behold.

Marjorie Pon, managing editorial, who shepherded the book along its way.

Madrid Tramble, production manager, who orchestrated the production from idea to printed book.

Nancy Tenney, copyeditor, who scrutinized every period, comma, and question mark.

INTRODUCTION

I am **BLACK AND BEAUTIFUL**, O **DAUGHTERS** of Jerusalem, like the tents of Kedar, like the curtains of Solomon. Do not gaze at me because I am ***dark,*** because the sun has gazed on me.

—Song of Solomon 1:5–6

I was urged to compile *Black Women in the Image of God* by my granddaughter Nandi, who helped me separate pictures for *Black Men in the Image of God,* the companion volume to this gift book. I wanted to honor the named and nameless women whose lives provide us with hope and victory, and I wanted to give Nandi a gift book that depicted the legacy of her people.

I belive that a people's strength is determined by the heart of women. Future generations depend on them to understand, mold, and change reality. In creation, no sex is superior to the other because God created all humankind. In the turbulence of this chaotic and unsympathetic world, women have met countless obstacles with courage and strength. Thus, *Black Women in the Image of God* is a celebration of truth created with powerful images and self-defining, inspirational words that show change and growth.

God made women from an ancient stillness to fill a void in the world. Women made a way out of no way, planting seeds of courage and hope. The names to the faces are not important. You know them. They have sailed across waters. They have planted fields of glory. They have raised a nation. They are our Nefertitis, Cleopatras, Nzingas, Big Mamas, Sisters, Cousins, Aunties, Girlfriends, and Sister-friends. *They are black and beautiful.*

Black Women in the Image of God is dedicated to women who maintain life with vision, direction, and hope; who lean on God knowing God's work is their work; who do not ask or need permission to think and act; who spread light through their beauty in thought and deed; who acquire spiritual power and unify humankind; who spread the virtues of peace, wisdom, and spirituality; and who love and are loved knowing that without love, life is meaningless.

Through this woven quilt of hope, life, and love, may you be blessed with the perseverance of these women. And may you be blessed with their determination so that you can prepare our daughters and sons for a better tomorrow.

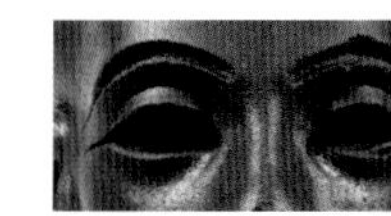

Then God said,
"Let us make humankind in our image,
according to our likeness;
and let them have dominion over . . .
the earth."
So God created humankind in God's image,
in the image of God, God created them;
male and female
created God them.

—Genesis 1:26–27

Amarna Sculpture, Egypt

KINSHIP WITH GOD

Are there no Shiphrahs, no Puahs among you, who will dare . . .
to refuse to obey the **WICKED LAWS** which require
man to enslave, to degrade, and to brutalize **WOMAN?**
Are there no Miriams, . . . no Huldahs . . .
Is there no *Esther* among you?

—Angelina E. Grimké

Divas Jo Thompson and Aretha Franklin

Opposite: *Aunt Violet Garmony*

I had a real kinship with God, and that's what has helped me pull out of the problems I've faced. Anybody who has kept up with my career knows that I've had my share of problems and trouble, but look at me today. . . . No matter how much success I achieved, I never lost my faith in God.

—Aretha Franklin

Everything in nature bespeaks the mother. The sun is the mother of the earth and gives nourishment of heat; it never leaves the universe at night until it has put the earth to sleep to the song of the sea and the hymn of the birds and brooks. And this earth is the mother of trees and flowers. It produces them, nurses them, and weans them. The trees and flowers become kind mothers of their great fruit and seeds. And the mother, the prototype of all existence, is the eternal spirit, full of beauty and love.

the eternal spirit

—Kahlil Gibran

4

KINSHIP WITH GOD

W. Grainger, Copper Engraving of Thomas Stothard's
Lost Painting *The Voyage of the Sable Venus*

it is dangerous for a woman to defy the gods,
to taunt them with the tongue's thin tip,
or shut in the weakness of mere humanity
or draw a line daring them to cross.

—Anne Spencer

defy the gods

Mike Colt, *Creation*

Opposite: *Mother and Child, Ghana*

grandmother EARTH

Grandmother Earth, Hear me!
The two leggeds,
the four leggeds,
the wingeds, and all that moves upon You
are Your children.
With all beings and all things
we shall be relatives; just as
we are related to you,
O Mother!

—Black Elk

MOST RELIGIONS SPEAK OF GOD IN THE MASCULINE GENDER. TO ME HE IS AS MUCH A MOTHER AS HE IS A FATHER. HE IS BOTH THE FATHER AND THE MOTHER IN ONE; AND WOMAN IS THE GOD-MOTHER. THE GOD-FATHER MAY BE REACHED THROUGH THE MIND OR THE IMAGINATION. BUT THE GOD-MOTHER CAN BE REACHED THROUGH THE HEART ONLY—THROUGH LOVE.

—Kahlil Gibran

woman is the god

Brenda Dendy Stroud, *Morning Glory*

The real power behind whatever success I have was something I found within myself—something that's in all of us . . . a little piece of God just waiting to be discovered.

—Tina Turner

divine

My father is time
my mother is nature
I am the
shimmering divine glow
of everlasting
light created in the
image of
God.
I am woman
born
from love's splendent vibrations
bronzed
by the fingertips of God.
Within me
are the invisible intangible seeds of the
Universe,
the intoxicating perfume flowing
from a waterless pool
to eternity.

—DOROTHY W. RILEY

Sophia LaCroix, *Sérénité*

Tonight I will sleep beneath your feet, O Lord of the mountains and valleys, ruler of the trees and vines. I will rest in your love, with you protecting me as a father protects his children, with you watching over me as a mother watches over her children. Then tomorrow the sun will rise and I will not know where I am; but I know that you will guide my footsteps.

—A Sioux Prayer

FAITH

I plunged into the job of creating something from nothing. . . . Though I hadn't a penny left, I considered cash money as the smallest part of my resources. I had faith in a living God, faith in myself, and a desire to serve.

—Mary McLeod Bethune

desire to serve

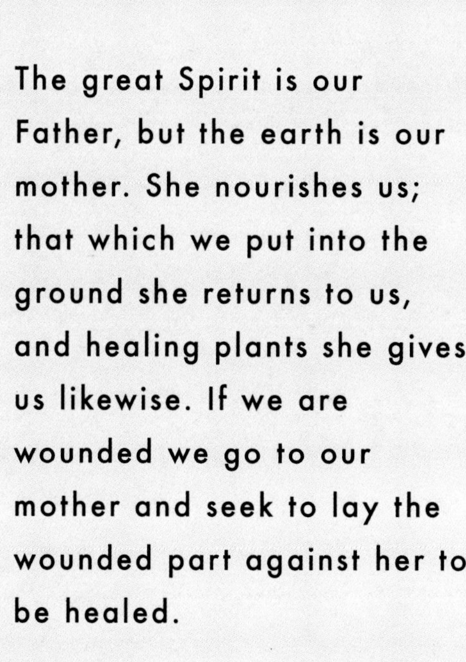

The great Spirit is our Father, but the earth is our mother. She nourishes us; that which we put into the ground she returns to us, and healing plants she gives us likewise. If we are wounded we go to our mother and seek to lay the wounded part against her to be healed.

—Big Thunder

HEAVEN IS AT YOUR MOTHER'S FEET

—Persian Proverb

I had to become a mother before I realized what a wonderful place in the scheme of things the Creator has given woman. She it is upon whom rests the jovial share of the *work of creation,* and I wonder if women who shirk their duties in that respect truly realize that they have not only deprived humanity of their contribution to perpetuity but that they have robbed themselves of one of the most **glorious** advantages in the development of their own **WOMANHOOD**.

—Ida B. Wells

William Johnson,
The Home Front

The home is depending upon her. . . . Man depends on her, sons and daughters are looking to her to find example, and God the Father is depending on her to be a light in the home, a peacemaker in the home, a helpmeet in the home, a councilor in the home.

depends on her

—Wood River Baptist Association Minutes

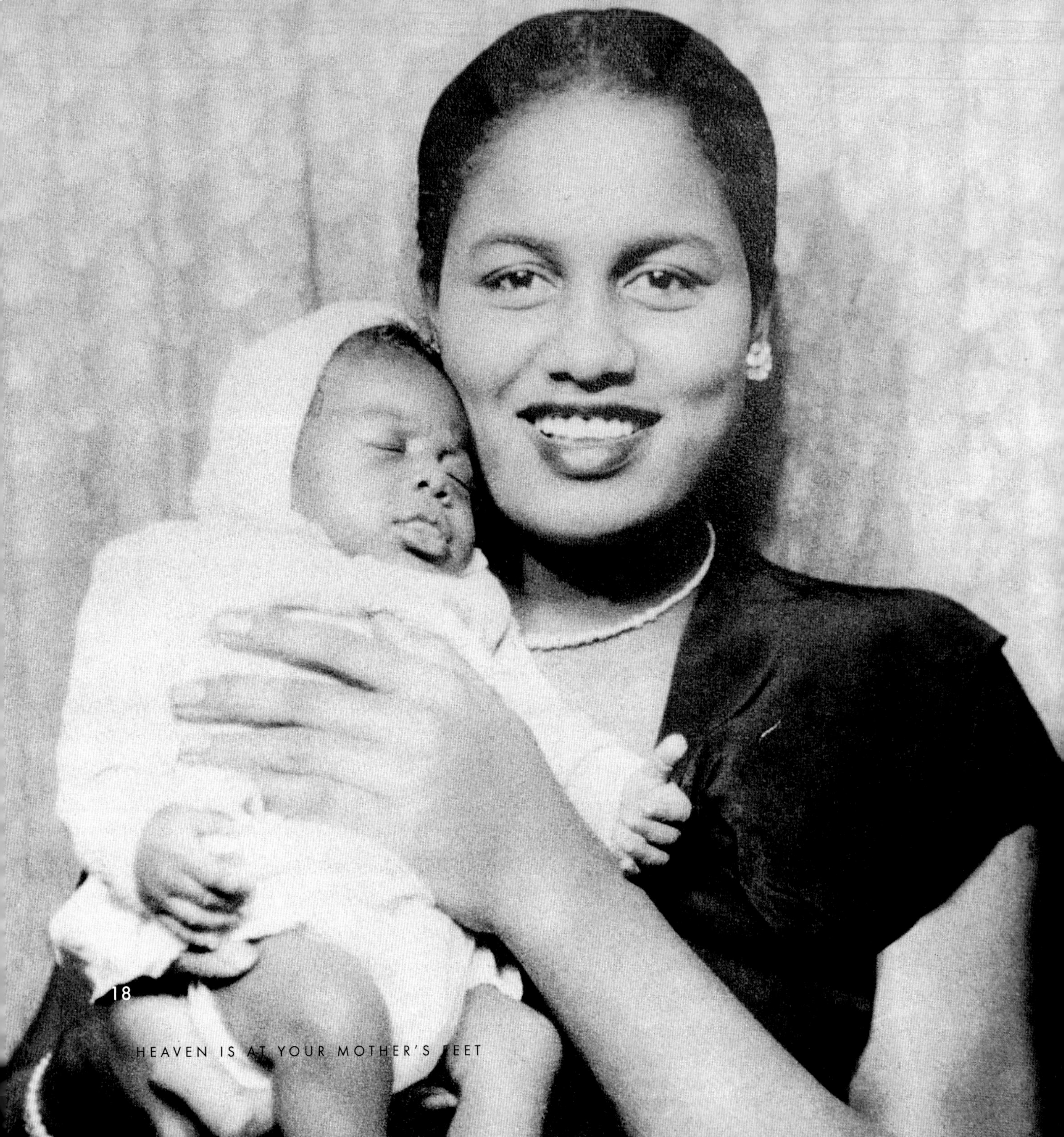

I am the vessel from whence you came
the lode filled with imaginings
aside from dreams my longings cannot
touch your reaching nor can I direct
your quest.

Your center is the earth the
cool continuum of mountain stream
the blasting winds
Nor can I follow there for I
am but bound flesh from whence you came

My private griefs are private griefs
and you will have your fill of such
I wish you joy and love and strength
a centering of mind and will
a homeward journey to your core
and when chaotic winds subside

an overflow of peace
a quiet soul

—MARI EVANS

Negro Woman Is 106

"Ninety-two," called one. "Ninety-seven," called another. Then came the astounding age of 106, which broke the record for the oldest in attendance at one of his programs, previously held by a woman in Sacramento, California, who was 105 years old.

From the stage to the middle of the auditorium arena went Breneman and Pierce to escort to the stage the oldest woman present—Mrs. Carrie Jackson, 1905 Angelique Street—a Negro woman who had been a slave and once had been sold for $600 at a sheriff's sale at Fayette, Missouri.

Mrs. Jackson, who celebrated her 106th birthday March 5, was born in Missouri, between Roanoke and Armstrong in Howard County. Her father came from Virginia and her mother from Kentucky, and she was the second-eldest of nine children. She was married to Alonzo Jackson the second year after the Civil War, and they were the parents of nine children, five of whom are living. Mr. Jackson died in 1936. She has 18 grandchildren, 11 great-grandchildren, and four great-great grandchildren.

—*Illinois State Journal,* March 6, 1954

Carrie Jackson, 106 Years Old

Grandma, I Love You

GRANDMOTHER

Grandma, I love you.
Remember the day you fried chicken for me?
We had mashed potatoes, biscuits, and
grape Kool-Aid.
Grandma, that was the best food I ever tasted.
Remember the day you took me
to the zoo?
That old goose flapped her wings and
scared me.
Grandma, you hugged me and
kissed me.
Grandma, I love you.
Grandma, I miss you.

I asked
why you had to go away.
Why couldn't you stay with me
until I was older?
I asked, where did you go?
Mama said
you were only on loan to us . . .
God loaned us one of His angels
to teach us about loving
and sharing
and giving
and learning
and growing
and changing
and going home
when time calls.

Grandma, I miss you.
Grandma, I love you.

—Tiaudra Riley

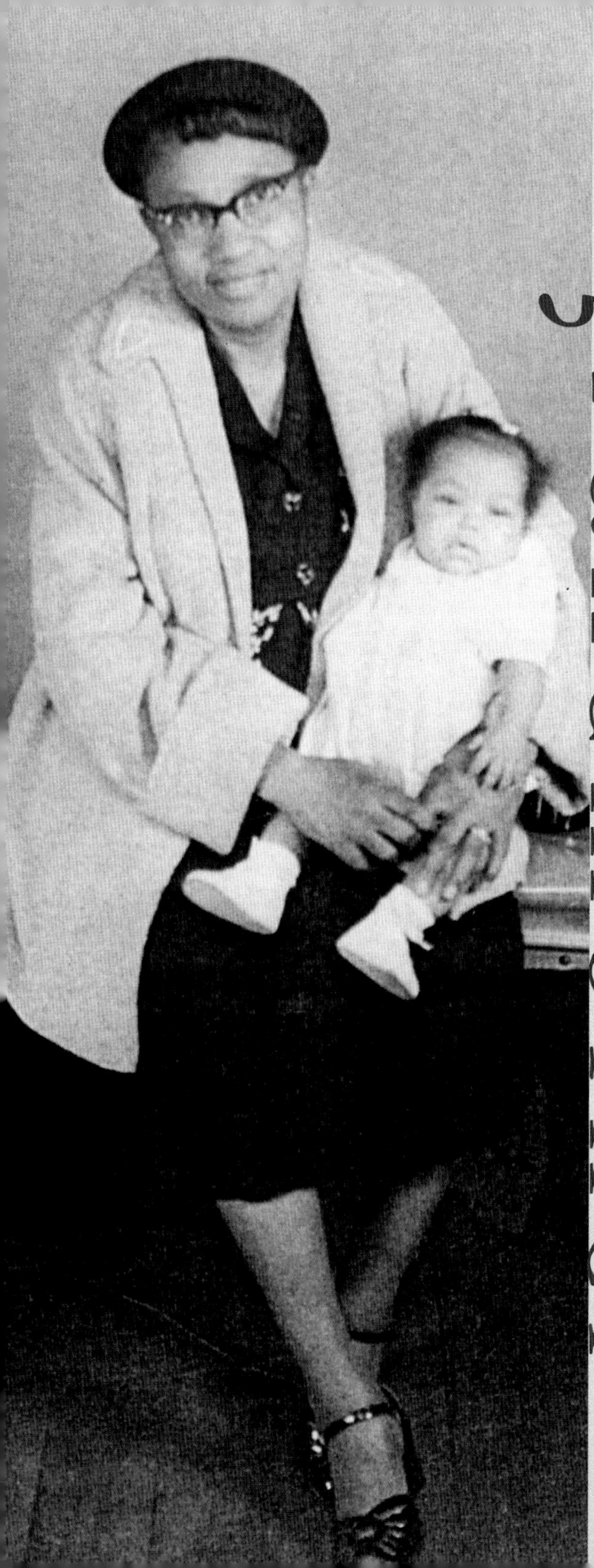

grandmother

your grandmother has

taught you this and you

want to ask your mother?

—Ivory Coast

Charlotte Summers and Granddaugther Charlotte Patricia Hil Carter

Opposite: *Juanita Hammond and Granddaughter Jocelyn Bush*

Mother is God number two.

—Malawi

SIMPLE THINGS

My grandmother taught me simple things like keeping your word, treating people the way you wanted to be treated. Traditional things that have stayed with me.

—Anfernee Hardaway

She was an incredible woman, not big, just a small woman with this great indomitable will. She was our shoulder to cry on, our sounding board, a dispenser of sage advice, our mother-confessor, our most honest and valued critic, and our staunchest defender.

—Johnnie Cochran

defender

Alcorn College Trio, c. 1918

DAUGHTERS OF AFRICA

Oh ye daughters of Africa, *awake! awake! arise!* No longer sleep nor slumber but distinguish yourselves. Show forth to the world that ye are endowed with noble and exalted faculties.

—Maria W. Stewart

Ain't no ocean, ain't no sea, keep my sister away from me. Me and you must never part. Me and you must have one heart.

—Alice Walker

La Shun Beal, *Sisters Forever*

daughter

SENATOR, I AM ONE OF THEM. YOU DO NOT SEEM TO UNDERSTAND WHO I AM. I AM A BLACK WOMAN, THE DAUGHTER OF A DINING-CAR WORKER. . . . IF MY LIFE HAS ANY MEANING AT ALL, IT IS THAT THOSE WHO START OUT AS OUT-CASTS CAN WIND UP AS PART OF THE SYSTEM.

—Patricia Roberts Harris

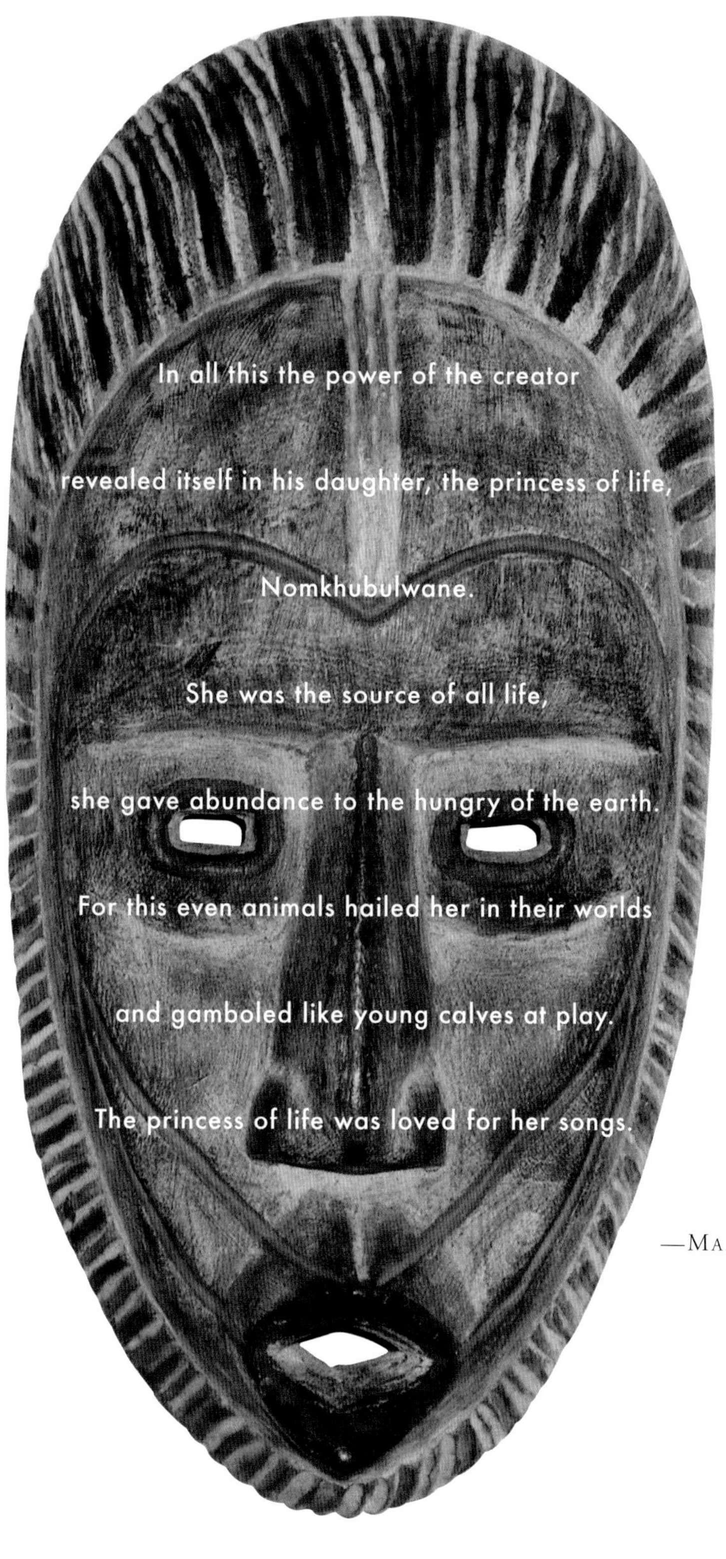

princess of life
princess of life
princess of life
princess of life

In all this the power of the creator
revealed itself in his daughter, the princess of life,
Nomkhubulwane.
She was the source of all life,
she gave abundance to the hungry of the earth.
For this even animals hailed her in their worlds
and gamboled like young calves at play.
The princess of life was loved for her songs.

—Mazisi Kunene

SISTERS

Cosmic African woman, mighty river
to whom all tributaries flow,
you are my pride and my delight.

From your varied faces emanates the splendor
of the rarest jewels of the universe—from the luminous
cool of pearl to the ruby's deepest radiance.

Daughters of a common land and sisters of the sun,
no matter where you flower, you are beautiful,
the ultimate creation of time and circumstance,

mysterious as an Egyptian cat, smooth
as a cowrie shell, colorful as a strip of kente cloth,
creative as braids of hair, ending and beginning

nowhere that can be defined, Cosmic African woman
of many faces, mighty river of my soul, my spirit flows
from you, returns forever to you
in an unbroken circle of love.

—Naomi Long Madgett

unbroken circle

you will never lose your daughter. it will be the one place that is always secure to place your foot, head, or heart. Don't hesitate to step. —Rhonda Ross

Daughters were to give mothers a sense of themselves.

—Sindamani Bridglal

Brenda Dendy Stroud, *Sisters*

sisterhood

If all we knew about sisterhood came from the sisterhood in us, then what would sisterhood look like, act like, and sound like? If there were no pledges to recite, no mottoes to repeat, no hymns of generations past, no prayers, no secret passwords, no songs to perform, if there were no ritual . . . If all we knew about sisterhood came from the sisterhood in us, then what would sisterhood look like?

—Vashti McKenzie

sister

They are your people sister; those who today speak your name.

we who from everywhere, from the water and the land . . .

speak no other name because fire does not die.

—Pablo Neruda

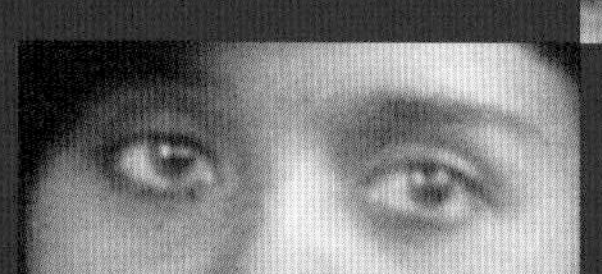

Brenda Dendy Stroud, *Bronzed Passion*

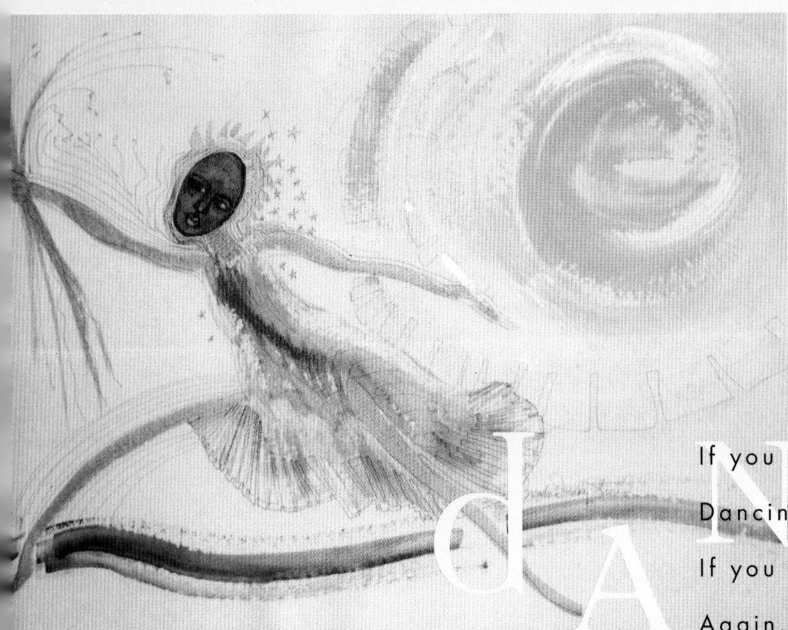

If you see a green snake

Dancing with your eldest daughter, it is I.

If you see a rainbow passionately embrace her,

Again, it is I.

I transform your eldest daughter into a rainbow

Behold her stalking with my seven serpents

Behold her shaking in the sunlight of my power

See her taste each of my sweet waters

See her kiss thrice my Damballah.

—Rene Despertes

You are a good daughter,
but a good daughter must be
a good wife.

—Buchi Emecheta

STRUGGLE FOR EXISTENCE

DON'T RIDE THE BUS to work, to town, to school or *anyplace* Monday, December 5. Another Negro woman has been arrested and put in jail because she refused to give up her bus seat. **DON'T RIDE THE BUSES** to work, to town, to school, or anywhere on Monday. If you work, take a cab, or share a ride, or walk. Come to a mass meeting, Monday at 7:00 p.m. at the Hall Street Baptist Church for further instruction.

—BIRMINGHAM, ALABAMA, FLYER, DECEMBER 5, 1955

BORN

I was not born with a silver spoon, it
was stainless steel.
I did not have stardust sprinkled in
my hair.

—Debbye Turner

silver spoon

struggle is eternal

I don't claim to have
a corner on an answer,
but I believe the
struggle is eternal.
Somebody else must
carry on.

—Ella Baker

Brenda Dendy Stroud, *After the Storm*

WOMEN

Women's problems cut across race and countries.

—Buchi Emecheta

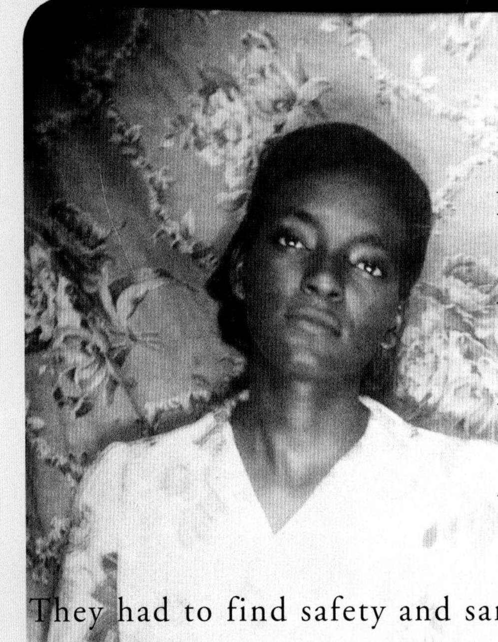

Black women whose ancestors were brought to the United States beginning in 1619 have lived through conditions of cruelties so horrible, so bizarre, the women had to re-invent themselves. They had to find safety and sanctity inside themselves or they would not have been able to tolerate those torturous lives. They had to learn to be self-forgiving quickly, for often their exterior exploits were at odds with their interior beliefs. Still they had to survive as wholly and healthily as possible in an infectious and sick climate.

re-invent

—Maya Angelou

I have always missed my mother all my life. All my life I have looked for her face, her love, her strength, her beauty on every American street. She was never there, but I have always carried her in my heart.

—Sonia Sanchez

special plight

The special plight and the role of black women is not something that just happened three years ago. We've had a special plight for 350 years.

—Fannie Lou Hamer

350 years

CHILDREN

R. Constantin, *The Garden Path*

We are the children of the sun are we
who write in the shadows of the evening,
who walk in the dark of the night,
who arise in the light of the dawn,
who go barefoot in the womb of the world, who sow the field,
who grow the daily bread,
who know the language of the wind,
who see the rain fall on a parched land and on tired faces,
who plough the furrows of the old,
who bring bones to bloom,
who consecrate bread in our flesh,
who break the chains and discover the way.

—Michele Najilis

and ain't I a woman?

Look at me! Look at my arms! I have plowed and planted, and gathered into barns, and no man could head me—and ain't I a woman? I could work as much and eat as much as a man (when I could get it) and bear de lash as well—and ain't I a woman? I have borne 13 children and seen 'em mos' all sold into slavery, and when I cried out with a mother's grief, none but Jesus heard—and ain't I a woman?

and ain't I a woman?

—Sojourner Truth

LOOK AT ME!

Brenda Dendy Stroud, *Celebration*

RHYTHM OF BEAUTY

Religion is very much like falling in love with a woman. You ***love*** her for her **COLOR** and the **MUSIC** and the **RHYTHM** of her—for her **BEAUTY,** which cannot be defined. There is no reason to it, there may be other women more gorgeously beautiful, but you love one and rejoice in her *companionship*.

—CLAUDE MCKAY

I honor the women of my race. Their beauty—their dark and mysterious beauty of midnight eyes, crumpled hair, and soft, full-featured faces. . . . No other woman on earth could have emerged from the hell of force and temptation which once engulfed and still surrounds black women in America with half the modesty and womanliness they retain.

BLACK

—W. E. B. DuBois

I came out of a tradition where those things are valued; where you talk about a woman with big legs and big hips and black skin. I came out of a black community where it was all right to have heavy hips and to be heavy. You didn't feel that people didn't like you. The values that infer you must be skinny come from another culture. Those are not the values that I was given by the women who served as my models. I refuse to be judged by the values of another culture. I am a black woman and I will stand as best I can in that imagery.

—Bernice Reagan

hips

Earl Jackson, *Shade All the Ground I Cover*

have you seen the
magic motion
that comes from
my hips
my big hips
my bow hips
my bedspring hips
my unrestrained-never-held-back-
keep-you-up-at-night
mama's hips
carrying me into
trouble and
out of it.
have you seen the
hypnotic switch of
my hips
my wide hips
my magnificent hips
my freedom-loving-traveling-
do-as-I-please
don't-you-wish-you-could-touch
Grandma hips
that makes you cut-your-eyes-
for-one-last-look at
my hips.

—Dorothy W. Riley

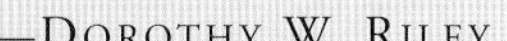

Jo Thompson

I never considered it a disadvantage to be a black woman. I never wanted to be anything else. We have brains. We are beautiful. We can do anything we set our minds to.

—Diana Ross

b e a u t i f u l

I must ease the tension in my heart

Gracious

I want to be more loving. Often there are good and sufficient reasons for exercising what seems a clean direct resentment. Again and again, I find it hard to hold in check the sharp retort, the biting comeback when it seems that someone has done violence to my self-respect and decent regard. How natural it seems to "give as good as I get," to "take nothing lying down," to announce to all and sundry in a thousand ways that "no one can run over me and get away with it!" All this is a part of the thicket in which my heart gets caught again and again. Deep within me, I want to be more loving—to glow with a warmth that will take the chill off the room which I share with those whose lives touch mine in the traffic of my goings and comings. I want to be more loving!

I want to be more loving in my heart! It is often easy to have the idea in mind, the plan to be more loving. To see it with my mind and give assent to the thought of being loving—that is crystal clear. But I want to be more loving in my heart! I must feel like loving; I must ease the tension in my heart that ejects the sharp barb, the stinging word. I want to be more loving in my heart so that, with unconscious awareness and deliberate intent, I shall be a kind, a gracious human being. Thus, those who walk the way with me may find it easier to live, to be gracious because of the Love of God which is increasingly expressed in my living.

"I want to be more loving in my heart!"

—Howard Thurman

loving

You
should
not
attempt
to
outwit
a woman.

—Alexandre Dumas

Mr. and Mrs. Sutton

Opposite: La Shun Beal, *Gracious*

You were the reason Adam ate the
apple and its core.
That when he left Eden, he left a
rich man.

—Toni Morrison

finding home

MOON

darkness

BLACK WOMAN

My hair is springy like the forest grasses
that cushion the feet of squirrels—
crinkled and blown in a south breeze
like the small leaves of native bushes.

My black eyes are coals burning
like a low, full jungle moon
through the darkness of being.
in a clear pool I see my face,
know my knowing.

My hands move pianissimo
over the music of the night:
gentle birds fluttering through leaves and grasses
they have not always loved,
nesting, finding home.

Where are my lovers?
Where are my tall, my lovely princes
dancing in slow grace
toward knowledge of my beauty?
Where
are my beautiful
black men?

—Naomi Long Madgett

seven stars
CAPRICES

It is easier by far to understand the seven stars than the caprices of a woman. For the ways of a woman are as changeable as the ways of the wind and beyond the understanding of seven Buddhas. A wise man attempts not to change the course of the wind.

—Melvin Tolson

Jonathan Green, *Daughters of the South*

A REGENERATIVE FORCE

uplift force

Black women are the regenerative force to **UPLIFT** the race.

—Lucy Craft Laney

nurture new life

NURTURE

lineage

Opposite: *Rita Blackwell*

The fact that I am a woman makes me the custodian of a new generation. It is a preordained role. Through me, others have life. I am an African woman, a link in a lineage that extends from the mists of the past into the blur of the unforeseen future. . . .

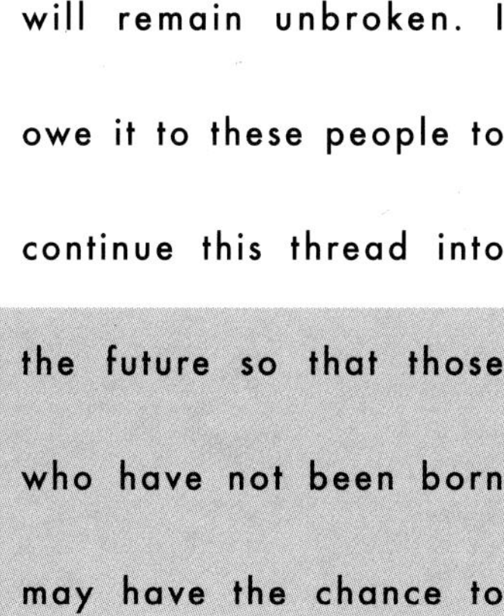

In this part of the world, it is expected that when her time comes, a woman will generate and nurture new life, thereby ensuring that the long and colorful lineage of people who once laughed, cried, and lived on this earth will remain unbroken. I owe it to these people to continue this thread into the future so that those who have not been born may have the chance to experience life.

—Juliana Omale

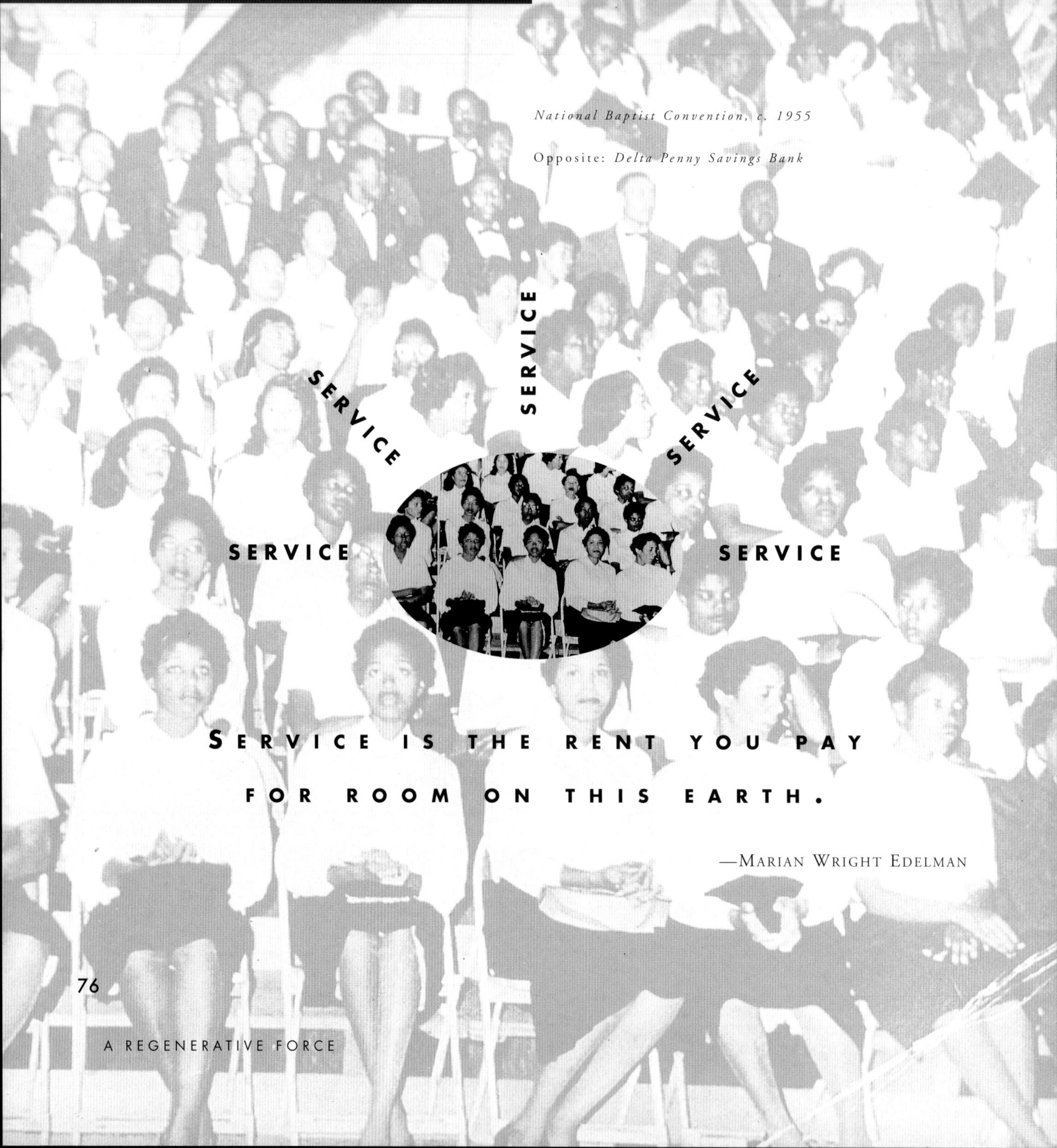

National Baptist Convention, c. 1955

Opposite: *Delta Penny Savings Bank*

SERVICE

SERVICE

SERVICE

SERVICE

SERVICE

SERVICE IS THE RENT YOU PAY FOR ROOM ON THIS EARTH.

—Marian Wright Edelman

what you were born to

do, you don't stop to

think should i? could i?

would i? i only think i

will? and i shall.

—Eva Jessye

PROGRESS

I became aware traveling recently through Africa and the Middle East, . . . usually the degree of progress can never be separated from the woman. If you're in a country that's progressive, the woman is progressive. If you're in a country that reflects the consciousness toward the importance of education it's because the woman is aware of the importance of education. But in every backward country where education is not stressed it's because the women don't have education. So one of the things I am convinced of is the importance of giving freedom to the woman, giving her education, and giving her incentive to put that same spirit and understanding in her children.

—MALCOLM X

Brenda Dendy Stroud,
Purpose of Life

the thirty-eighth year
of my life,
plain as bread
round as cake
an ordinary woman

an ordinary woman

I had expected to be
smaller than this
more beautiful
wiser in africkan ways,
more confident
I had expected
more than this.

I will be forty soon
my mother once was forty

my mother died at forty-four
a woman of sad counte-
    nance
leaving behind a girl
awkward as a stork
her hair was a jungle and
she was very wise
and beautiful
and sad.
I have dreamed dreams
to you mama
more than once
I have wrapped me in your
    skin
and made you live again,
more than once
I have taken the bones you
    hardened
and built daughters
and they blossom and
    promise fruit
like africkan bees.
I am a woman now
an ordinary woman.

in the thirty-eighth
year of my life
surrounded by life
a perfect picture of
blackness blessed
I had not expected this
loneliness.

it is western
it is the final
europe in my mind,
in the middle of my life
I am turning the final turn
into the shining dark
let me come to it whole
and holy
not afraid
not lonely
out of my mother's life
into my own
into my own.

I had expected more than
    this
I had not expected to be
an ordinary woman.

—LUCILLE CLIFTON

STRENGTH

women are blessed

with a jewel of

strength that glows

all the time.

—JUDITH JAMISON

Opposite: *"Brownie Camera"*

When people made up their minds that they wanted to be free and took action, then there was a change. But they couldn't rest on just that change. It has to continue.

—Rosa Parks

Elwyn Bush, *Marian Anderson*

KIND OF IMPRESSION

I suppose I might insist on making issues of things. But that is not my nature, and I always bear in mind that my mission is to leave behind me the kind of impression that will make it easier for those who will follow.

—Marian Anderson

When you civilize a man, you only civilize an individual, but when you civilize a woman, you civilize a whole people.

—Patrice Lumumba

a whole people

ORACLE OF MY HEART

ORACLE OF MY HEART, with breasts like tangerines, to me *you* are more tasty than crab-stuffed aubergines, you are the tripe in my pot, the dumplings in my peas, my *intoxicating* herbal tea. You are the salted beef over which my heart stands guard, the syrupy crumpet that oozes in my throat. You are the piping-hot dish, mushrooms and rice, crispy fried potatoes and crackling fish. . . . My love's **cravings** follow you wherever you go.

—EMILE ROUMER

women who build nations

learn

to love

men

who build nations

learn to love

children

building sand castles

by the rising sea.

—Audre Lorde

African Bride

Opposite: *Georgia Mae Kirkland*

BUILD NATIONS

LOVE

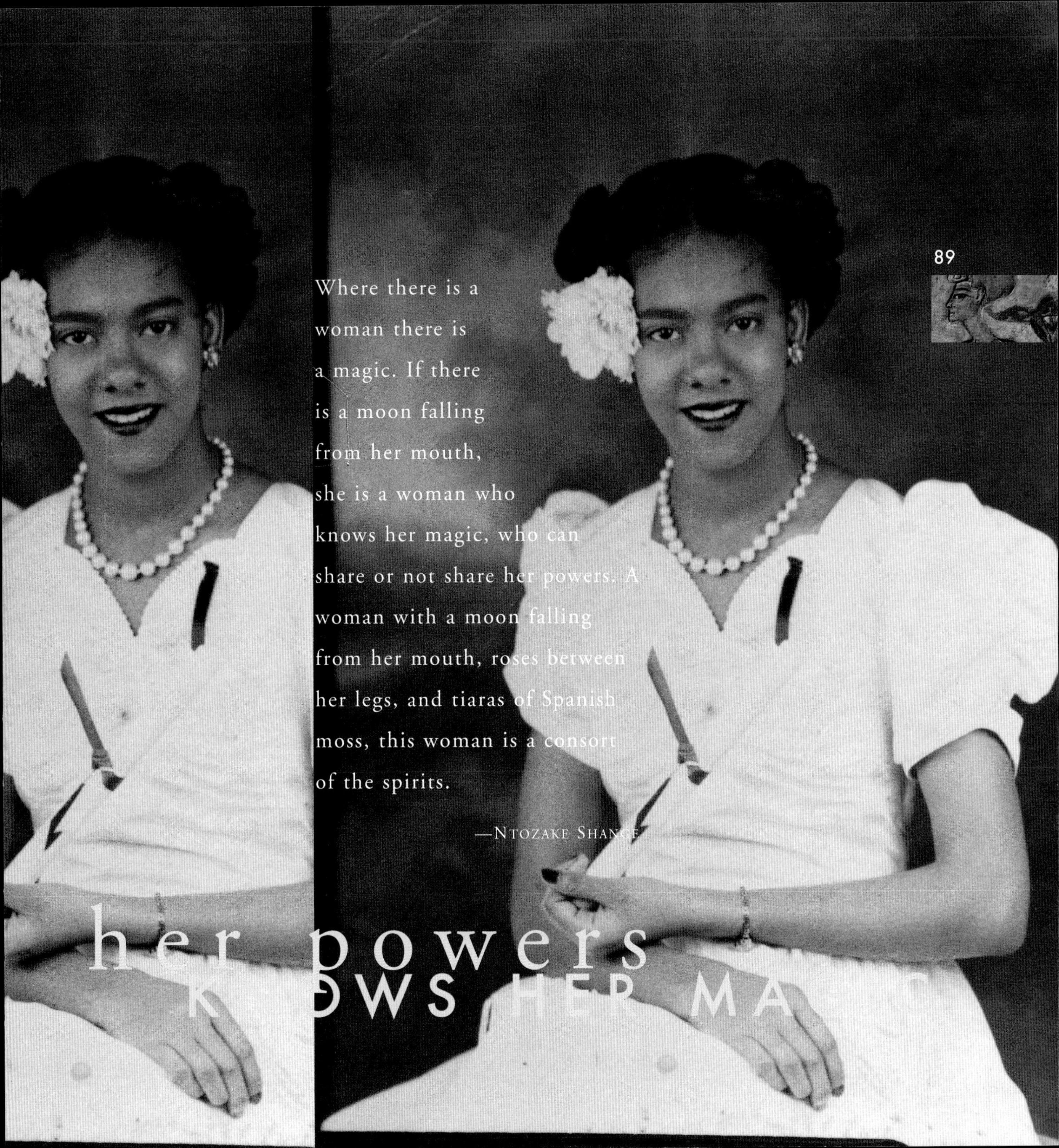

Where there is a
woman there is
a magic. If there
is a moon falling
from her mouth,
she is a woman who
knows her magic, who can
share or not share her powers. A
woman with a moon falling
from her mouth, roses between
her legs, and tiaras of Spanish
moss, this woman is a consort
of the spirits.

—Ntozake Shange

her powers

KNOWS HER MAGIC

SHE CAPTURES ME WITH HER EYES

How well she knows to cast the noose,
And yet not pay the cattle tax!
She casts the noose on me with her hair,
She captures me with her eye;
She curbs me with her necklace,
She brands me with her seal ring.

—From Papyrus Chester Beatty

blesses his life

. . . who both blesses his life and makes him wish he had never been born.

never been born

—Toni Morrison

She does more for me than all medicines

Her coming to me is my amulet,

The sight of her makes me well.

When she opens her eyes my body is young

Her speaking makes me strong

Embracing her expels my malady

Seven days since she went from me.

—From Papyrus Chester Beatty

what she does to me?

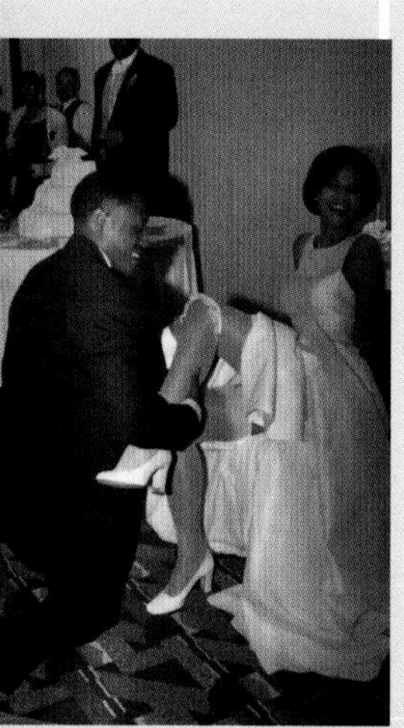

If I have a headache, I have myself bled.

If I have a colic, I take some medicine.

If I am seized by the pox, I go down to the Hot-Springs.

But where is there help, for what she does to me?

—Ethiopia

Opposite: Earl Jackson, *Where Paths Meet*

turn to each other in QUIET affection

Let us turn to each
other in quiet
affection,
walk in peace to the
edge of old age.
And I shall be with you
each unhurried day.

—EGYPT

LIBERATE MY SOUL

O my Beloved!

Take me,

Liberate my soul,

Fill me with love,

and release me from both worlds.

When I set my heart on anything but you

a fire burns me from inside.

O my Beloved!

Take away what I want,

Take away what I do,

Take away everything,

that takes me from you.

—Jalaluddin Rumi

CLASS
OF
97

LEADING US TO THE SUNRISE

My dear *daughters*,

You are leaders to guide our nation,

I WANT TO FOLLOW YOU.

Unashamed,

with all my strength,

exploding burning righteous resentment.

I'm determined to **FOLLOW YOUR PATH.**

—KO-UN

Maggie Ann Buckingham Sweetner, c. 1933

Opposite: *Congressman Adam Clayton Powell, Mrs. Powell, and Adam Clayton Powell III*

GIFTED

I've always known I was gifted, which is not the easiest thing in the world for a person to know, because you're not responsible for your gift, only for what you do with it.

—Hazel Scott

Opposite: *St. Mary's School*

YOU SOW
you reap

You sow a thought, you reap an action.

You sow an action, you reap a character.

You sow a character, you reap a destiny.

—Marva Collins

if you really want to be powerful, if you really want to be influential, and if you really want people to support you, then just serve. I'm powerful because I am a serving woman.

—Reverend Willie Barrow

Opposite: *Shirley Chisholm and Al Dunmore*

HOPE & change

I AM BY DEFINITION—A DIFFERENT KIND OF SENATOR.

I AM AN AFRICAN AMERICAN, A WOMAN, A PRODUCT OF THE WORKING CLASS.

I CANNOT ESCAPE THE FACT THAT I COME TO THE SENATE AS A SYMBOL OF HOPE AND CHANGE. NOR WOULD I WANT TO BECAUSE MY PRESENCE IN AND OF ITSELF WILL CHANGE THE U.S. SENATE.

—CAROL MOSELEY-BRAUN

Jamal Jones, *Determination*

Opposite: *Miss Gibbs, Dr. Coles, and Dr. Gibbs*

I WILL NOT LET YOU FAIL.

—Marva Collins

If we do nothing to improve
our world,
then we cannot call ourselves
educated women.

—Johnnetta B. Coles

improve our world

Donald Calloway, *In Touch with the Spirit*

Opposite: *The Seed Sprouts*

When she walked into a house
she had only to sniff the air for a few seconds
to absorb the climate,
feel the invisible presences,
capture the signs of misfortune,
divine the dreams,
hear the whispers of the dead,
and comprehend the needs of the living.

—Isabel Allende

Tomorrow there will be more to do, and failure waits for those who stay with some success made yesterday. Tomorrow you must try once more and even harder than before.

—Marcia Fudge

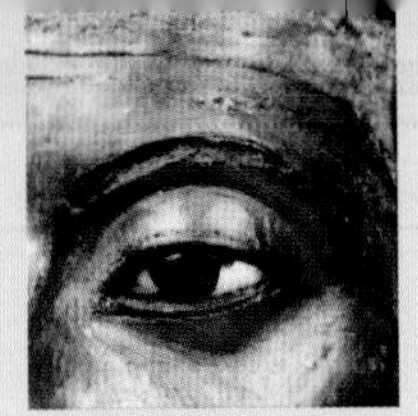

I am smitten with the love of wisdom, and I am constrained by the cords of understanding; for wisdom is far better than treasure of gold and silver, and wisdom is the best of everything that has been created on the earth. It is sweeter than honey, brings more joy than wine, illumines more than the sun, is more precious than jewels. She causes the ears to hear and the heart to comprehend. I love her like a mother and she embraces me as her own child. I will follow her footprints and she will not cast me away.

WITH THE LOVE

—Queen Makeda

OF WISDOM

equatorial

CIRCLE

serpent

with the equatorial circle
tied around her waist like a
small world
the black woman, a new woman,
advances in her sheer serpent's
gown.

—Nicolas Guillen

SOURCES

Photographs courtesy of: Regina Baker (p. 27), Jacqueline Sweetner Caffey (pp. 14, 26, 32, 47, 51, 67, 101, 102), Falana Carter, (pp. 24, 75), Sandra Malone Goudy (p. 92), Diane Walker Hall (pp. 10, 13, 28, 37, 43, 71, 82, 91, 103, 109), Juanita Hammonds (pp. 10, 21, 25), Anita Harrell (p. 18), Emma Heywood (pp. 44, 56, 96), Beatrice Johnson (pp. 12, 40, 50, 69, 70, 71, 89), Jeremy and Lisa Lincoln (p. 94), Shirley Lusby (pp. 76, 93), Sherlin McNeal (pp. 12, 23, 52, 60, 78), Dorothy Winbush Riley (pp. 22, 34, 46, 61, 74, 77, 83, 88, 107, 112), Schiavi Riley (pp. 17, 36, 46), Tiaudra Riley (pp. 3, 98), and Jo Thompson (pp. 2, 65, 100, 104).

Poetry and prose: Lucille Clifton, "The 38th Year," copyright 1987 by Lucille Clifton. Reprinted from *Good Woman: Poems and a Memoir 1969–1980 by Lucille Clifton* with permission of BOA Edition, Ltd., Rochester, New York. @ Mari Evans, excerpt from "Ode to My Sons," used by permission of the author. @ Naomi Long Madgett, "Black Woman," from *Pink Ladies in the Afternoon* (Lotus Press) and "Sisters of the Sun," used by permission of the author. @ Tiaudra Riley, "Grandma, I Love You," used by permission of the author. @ Howard Thurman, "I Want to Be More Loving," from *Meditations of the Heart,* by Howard Thurman. Copyright 1981 by Howard Thurman. Used by permission of the Howard Thurman Foundation.

Art: La Shun Beal, *Sisters Forever,* acrylic on canvas, 30" x 40", private collection, and *Gracious,* acrylic on canvas, 16" x 20", private collection, used by permission of the artist. @ Elwyn Bush, *Bust of Marian Anderson,* terra cotta, 18" high, collection of Juanita Hammonds, used by permission of the artist. @ Donald Calloway, *In Touch with the Spirit,* watercolor on paper, 12" x 18", used by permission of the artist. @ Mike Colt, *Creation,* acrylic on canvas, 30" x 40", used by permission of the artist. @ R. Constantin, *The Garden Path,* acrylic on canvas, 16" x 18". @ Jonathan Green, *Daughters of the South,* 1993, oil on canvas, 72" x 72", copyright 1993 Jonathan Green Studios, Naples, Florida. Used by permission. @ *Head of Queen Tiye,* late reign of Amenhotep III—Akhenaten, used by permission of the Agyptisches Museum, Berlin, Germany, 21834. @ Earl Jackson, *Shade All the Ground I Cover,* oil on canvas, 24" x 36", and *Where Paths Meet,* oil on canvas, 24" x 36", used by permission of the artist. @ William Henry Johnson, *The Home Front,* oil on plywood, 39.5" x 31.24", Aaron Douglas Collection, Amistad Research Center, New Orleans, Louisiana. Used by permission. @ Jamal Jones, *Determination,* oil on canvas, 24" x 36", used by permission of the artist. @ Sophia LaCroix, *Sérénité,* 1995, oil on canvas, 18" x 14", collection of Dr. and Mrs. Thys, used by permission of the artist. @ *Painted Relief of a King and Queen,* late period, year 15 or later, used by permission of the Agyptisches Museum, Berlin, Germany, 15000. @ *A Princess,* middle to late period, used by permission of the Agyptisches Museum, Berlin, Germany, DDR21223. @ Brenda Dendy Stroud, *Celebration,* 1996, mixed media; *Morning Glory,* mixed media; *After the Storm,* mixed media; *Purpose of Life,* mixed media; *Sisters,* 1996; *Bronzed Passion,* used by permission of the artist. @ Thomas Stothard, *The Voyage of the Sable Venus,* 1801, used by permission of the British Library, 1005565.011.

KINSHIP WITH GOD

HEAVEN IS AT YOUR MOTHER'S FEET

DAUGHTERS OF AFRICA

STRUGGLE FOR EXISTENCE

RHYTHM OF BEAUTY

A REGENERATIVE FORCE

ORACLE OF MY HEART

LEADING US TO THE SUNRISE